ANCESTRAL ECHOES OF YULE

ACTIVITIES FOR THE FAMILY TO BRING CONNECTION THROUGH CELEBRATION AND EMBODYING THE WINTER SEASON

SHELLEY KAMPF

First published in 2024 by Shelley Kampf

ISBN 978-1-7635874-0-3

Text copyright and illustrations Shelley Kampf 2024
The right of Shelley Kampf to be identified as the author and illustrator of the work has been asserted by her in accordance with the Copyright, Designs and Patent Act 1988.

All rights reserved. No part of this publication may be reproduced, stored in a retrieval system, or transmitted, in any form or by any means (electronic, mechanical, photocopying, recording or otherwise), without the prior written permission of Shelley Kampf.

Design by Shelley Kampf

Printed and bound by IngramSparks

WHEN WE REMEMBER WHERE WE HAVE COME FROM, WE CAN SEE WHERE WE ARE GOING.

Thank you to my three beautiful children for always lighting the way.
Thank you to my Mother for bringing me in to this world and all the proof reading you have done!
A big thank you to my "editor" and friend, Sarah for all the time, effort and support you have given me, I am truly grateful!
And to all my friends and family for supporting my journey,
Love to you all.

Even as I child I remember questioning the absurdity of celebrating winter in the middle of summer being in the southern hemisphere. My dad brought his traditions from America, and so we were the only kids that celebrated Halloween on October 31st, which has now become a popular tradition. But it always felt off, and it was always too hot to be in costumes! I was missing crucial reverence of what these celebrations were about, and celebrating them in the opposite season just added to the confusion. I muddled through the years, always looking for something more spiritual to nurture. I had a deep knowing of something missing, but was still going along with the norm. It was my first child's second Christmas; I was putting up the Christmas tree in the heat, dripping with sweat, and I lost it. WHAT ARE WE DOING? I questioned and vowed that I wasn't doing it again, and that moment started my own journey of delving deep into the ancestral knowledge of these celebrations. There wasn't a lot out there, especially how to bring this reverence of the seasons to our children, in order for it to become second nature to them as it once would have been. I grieved. I still grieve for the lost knowledge of our ancestors, and the security of having elders to call on. I wanted someone to guide my way, and light my path in the ways of nature. As I began my journey into celebrating the seasons, my friends wanted to know what I had learned and how to share this knowledge with their own children. It takes a lot of strength to swim against the current, but once I started it got easier and became our new normal. My husband had a hard time transitioning for fear our kids were missing out, which is totally understandable! Once you start you will see you are not missing out, but adding so much more. The feeling of alignment with the seasons is so nourishing and all those fond childhood memories of tradition are enhanced. These celebrations now sit so much deeper within our family, as they make sense and feel comfortable. I don't know about you but for me, putting a tree up and trying to cook a roast in the middle of summer is my idea of torture! When we can really ground ourselves into what we are sharing with our kids, it gives us the strength to be leaders and move in the direction that is authentic to us. Maybe you are lucky enough to know your ancestry and can trace your origins back to homelands. If so, find what suits you; explore which characters feel right to you and bring these new traditions into your home. I hope that this book can light your way to a more nourishing way to celebrate winter with your loved ones.

X Shelley

HOW TO USE THIS BOOK

I'm so thrilled that you have chosen to bring some magic and connection into your family with my book! I have designed the book to inspire and bring connection to your family while doing these activities. Alternatively, the book can assist you in creating your own individual countdown towards Yule. In the back of the book, you will find print outs (if you own the eBook), or cut outs (if you own a hard copy). I give you full permission to cut into the book, or if you are like me and hesitate to cut a book, photocopy and print. There are further instructions on how to set up your countdown on page 50. You will also find songs at the back of the book to sing together around a fire or on a lantern walk. I trust that you will use your own discretion and common sense regarding safety while participating in these activities. Most importantly, enjoy your winter celebrations with your family and friends! I would love to see and hear how you have used the book. Please stay in touch through my website: shelleykampf.com

CONTENTS

CONNECTION..11

    ORIGINS OF THE YULE TREE 12

    DECORATING THE TREE 14

    LETTER TO SANTA 15

    A LITTLE ABOUT SANTA 16

    YULE LOG 18

    YULETIDE 19

    RANDOM ACTS OF KINDNESS 20

    HIKE 21

    WINTER GATHERING 22

CHARADES..23-25

CRAFT..26

    PAPER CHAIN 27

    SNOW FLAKES 28

    ORANGE POMANDER 29

    WRAPPING PAPER 30

    YULE CARDS 31

    CRACKERS 32

    WREATH 33

    TIN CAN LANTERN 34

    GLASS JAR LANTERN 35

    YULE FAIRIES AND ELVES 36

CONTENTS

RECIPES..40

ELDERBERRY SYRUP 41

GINGERBREAD PANCAKES 42

GINGERBREAD COOKIES 43

WINNIE'S APPLE CRUMBLE 44

STAINED GLASS WINDOW COOKIES 45

HOT CHOCOLATE 46

SPICED MEAD 47

GIFTS..48

ROCKY ROAD 50

TALLOW CREAM 51

SALVE 52

HANGING ORNAMENTS 53

FIRE LIGHTERS 54

ROLLED CANDLES 55

POURED CANDLES 56

COUNTDOWN 57-61

SONGS 62-66

CONNECTIONS

ORIGINS OF THE YULE TREE

It is a beloved symbol of the winter season, and it sparks excitement and anticipation. The Yule Tree has deeply rooted ancestral traditions. In Norse mythology, an evergreen such as fir or pine represented fertility and endurance. It also promised the return of spring; it's colour symbolised the survival of life through the harsh winter months. During the twelve days of celebration our ancestors would bring evergreen trees into their homes, and decorate them with candles, fruits, and nuts. These decorations were added to ward off evil spirits and celebrate the rebirth of the sun, It was believed that these decorations would bring blessings for the coming year and protect the home from malevolent spirits. Similarly, the Celts believed that the winter solstice marked the time when the Oak King (representing the waxing year and the return of the sun's strength), triumphed over the Holly King (symbolizing the waning year and the reign of darkness). The Yule Tree, often an oak or holly tree adorned with seasonal greenery, represents the victory of light over darkness and the promise of warmer days ahead. Decorating the Yule Tree with sacred symbols, such as sun wheels, Celtic knots, and animal ornaments, was believed to bring blessings and protection to the household. Burning Yule logs made from oak or other sacred woods was a common practice, and symbolised the return of light and warmth to the world.

As we became woven together, the Yule Tree became Christianised. It began to symbolise the light of Christ and the hope of salvation, and so it was renamed the Christmas tree. In the 19th century, Queen Victoria and Prince Albert popularised the Yule tree, by displaying a decorated Christmas tree at Windsor Castle, which led to its widespread adoption as an integral part of Christmas celebrations in Europe and North America. Unfortunately, by then we had forgotten what the origins of the Yule Tree was. However, I feel that somewhere deep in our bones haven't forgotten, and we continue to have the memories of our ancestors and the comfort of cycling nature around us. In both Norse and Celtic traditions, the Yule Tree symbolised the enduring spirit of life, the cyclical nature of the seasons, and the hope for renewal and abundance in the coming year. The Yule tree still remains a cherished symbol of the holiday season, bringing joy, warmth, and a sense of tradition to homes and communities worldwide. Whether adorned with ornaments, lights, or cherished family heirlooms. The Yule Tree continues to symbolize hope, renewal, and the enduring spirit of the season and natural cycles of the earth. All this just does not make sense in the middle of summer if you are living in the Sothern hemisphere. When we relearn and start to remember our heritage that impowers us to make choices and choose what traditions we want to inherit.

DECORATING THE YULE TREE

Decorating the Yule tree is one of my favourite activities. The excitement of selecting a tree and digging out the decorations that have been in storage for a year. Your Yule tree doesn't have to be extravagant; it could be a small cut branch, or a pot plant or an artificial tree or a tree that is as tall as the celling, because we all know that guy that goes big! (Thanks Dads). A real tree is always nice, as it adds the fresh scent of pine to the house, but sometimes it's not practical and an artificial one will do the job. Whichever tree you choose, pop some festive music on (my favourite is the Nutcracker) and start bringing out your decorations. Each year that you create more will build memories of years and ages past. Let go of perfection, and marvel in the smiles of confidence and feeling of belonging your children will experience through the process of decorating the tree.

- Paper
- Pens, pencils, felt pens
- Endless imagination

LETTER TO SANTA

There's a certain enchantment woven into the act of writing a letter to Santa Claus. It's a rite of passage; a timeless tradition that carries with it a sense of wonder, innocence, and anticipation. Dreams take shape in children's minds as their wishes take flight; up they go with the smoke through the chimney, or maybe they are placed in the letter box, and magically find their way to Santa. These letters carry the belief in magic and the possibility of miracles. It's a reminder that when we believe and bring magic into our lives, anything is possible. It is so special to have some insight into what your children ask for, and to see their faces light up during their imaginative play. Younger ones may need to dictate to you, but once they are able, let them go wild writing their letter themselves. There are no limits; get fancy with decorations or keep it simple with a plain old letter and a fun stamp. Don't forget to take a picture to remember the sweetness of the years gone by.

A LITTLE ABOUT SANTA.

The timeless and customary figure of generosity has blended over time with ancestral traditions, myths, folklore and customs of a timeless figure of generosity and other female figures into what to create the character we recognise today as Santa. In Celtic mythology the Green Man is a symbol of fertility, rebirth, and the cycle of nature. Santa is described as a figure with a face surrounded by leaves or foliage; this reminds us of the vitality of the natural world. Perhaps originally, Santa's suit was green? Coca-Cola advertisements and the story 'The Night Before Christmas' has shaped this beloved figure into a big jolly man in a red suit. In Nordic folklore, Odin is the wise and benevolent god associated with wisdom, magic, and poetry. He has a resemblance to Santa Claus, but instead of reindeer, Odin rode through the night sky on an eight-legged horse named Sleipnir. During the winter solstice, he was said to have led the Wild Hunt , rewarding those who showed hospitality and generosity, and punishing those who did not. Some aspects of Odin's mythology, such as his long white beard and association with gift-giving, likely influenced the development of Santa Claus in northern European cultures. Frau Holda or Mother Hulda, a Norse goddess, was associated with winter, spinning, and domestic tasks. In folklore, she is often depicted as a kindly old woman who rewards hard work and punishes laziness. During the winter solstice, it's believed that Holda travels through the land, bestowing gifts upon those who have been diligent and industrious; maybe she helped inspire our current-day Mrs Clause?

Saint Nicholas was a Christian bishop who lived in the 4th century in the area now known as Turkey. Saint Nicholas was known for secretly giving gifts to the needy, and leaving sweets in children's shoes. Over time, the stories of his benevolence spread throughout Europe, and became intertwined with various local customs and celebrations. In artic folklore, the reindeer goddess Beiwe rides through the sky in a sleigh pulled by reindeer, bringing the sun back to the world after the long polar night. Her reindeer are said to have golden antlers that shine with the light of the sun.

Other stories say that the reindeer carry the sun it their antlers, which symbolises the return of warmth, light and fertility to the land. I will also add here that Dasher, Prancer, Vixen and the others were originally female reindeer, not males as people now believe. We know this, as male reindeer shed their antlers during winter time . As all of these stories have weaved together, we have lost our tribal beginnings. Throw in thousands of years of patriarchal society, and we now have what we all recognise as Santa: the big jolly guy in red. The name Santa is most likely derived from Saint, a Christian name. Choose a name that you and your family feel comfortable with. We have stuck with the name Santa as it's a household name and creates less confusion.

YULE LOG

- Twine
- Dried citrus
- Dried herbs
- Cinnamon sticks
- Written blessings

The Yule log is one of my favourite things to do for Yule. The process of my husband and kids going out, choosing and cutting a log, and then decorating it and of course the burning. The Yule log was typically a large, specially selected log, often from a hardwood tree like oak or ash. It was chosen for its ability to burn slowly, and provide warmth throughout the long winter night. The log was traditionally harvested with great care, and ceremonially decorated before being brought into the home. The lighting of the Yule log was a central ritual of the Yule celebration. It was usually kindled from the remains of the previous year's Yule log, which symbolises the continuity of the seasons and the cyclical nature of life. The lighting of the Yule log was accompanied by prayers, invocations or blessings, which were believed to invoke the blessings of the gods and spirits for the coming year. Once lit, the Yule log would burn throughout the night, symbolising the return of the sun, and the triumph of light over darkness. It was believed that keeping the Yule log burning all night would bring luck, prosperity, and protection to the household for the coming year. It was also believed that the ashes from the Yule log had magical properties and were scattered over fields or gardens to ensure a bountiful harvest in the coming year. Gather your log and decorations and let's get started! Think about where you will burn the log - will it be outside or in the fireplace? Select one that will be a suitable size for your fire place or alternative safe burning area. Create a bundle of dried herbs and cinnamon sticks, and if you would like to, you can also add a written blessing. Tie the bundle with twine to secure it together. I like to add a piece of dried citrus to the knot, as the citrus wheel symbolises the sun and the circle of the year. You may like to do a bundle for each family member, or just do one to share. Once you have your bundles together, it is time to tie them to the log. Now your log is ready to be burnt on Yule Day.

YULETIDE

It's the big day; early morning excitement and cheer abound! It is the shortest day and longest night of the year. It's a time when the sun reaches its lowest point in the sky and begins its gradual ascent toward longer days, and the promise of spring. Yule is a momentous occasion in ancestral culture, signifying the triumph of light over dark ness, and the turning point in the cycle of the seasons. It is where all the rituals leading up to Yule come to fruition, with feasting and gatherings. These are aimed at welcoming the return of the sun, and ensuring fertility, prosperity and protection for the coming year. Music, dance and storytelling are important components of Yule celebrations; as you come together, share in the joy and camaraderie of the season. Sing songs, play music and dance. Tell tales of family, heroes, and magical creatures around the fire. Prepare a feast together: bring connection through the generations, by passing down recipes and skills . Feasting was and is a central part of Yule festivities, with abundant food and drink being shared among family and friends. Boar, a symbol of fertility and prosperity, was a common centrepiece of the Yule feast. In our family we have created the tradition of the Yule log cake, an expected tradition that is waited for with anticipation. Yule is also the day of gift-giving and exchanging tokens of goodwill and hospitality with loved ones. Celebrating Yule is a meaningful and enriching experience, as you honour the cycles of nature and come together in celebration during the darkest time of the year. Many blessings for you and your family on this day as you embody and bring reverence for the winter season.

RANDOM ACTS OF KINDNESS

Within Yule lies an invitation for us to share kindness to those around us, illuminating others' lives with generosity and compassion. These acts don't need to be extravagant; it is often the smallest gestures that leave the most lasting impressions – a smile to a stranger, a handwritten note of appreciation, baking cookies for a neighbour, or a simple act of service for someone in need. These acts send a ripple effect through lives, effecting whole communities. By extending a helping hand, we inspire others to do the same, initiating a chain reaction of generosity and compassion that strengthens the bonds connecting us all. Helping our friends and neighbours gives us an opportunity to foster bonds of friendship and goodwill, thereby building stronger, more resilient communities where everyone feels supported. If we can show our children what a supported community looks like, we can have hope that that ripple effect will continue on for many generations to come. Therefore, in the spirit of Yule, let us embrace the opportunity to spread kindness far and wide. Let's remember those who may feel lonely or overlooked and reach out to them with gestures of friendship and love. Let's extend a helping hand, sharing our blessings with those in need. And let's strive to cultivate an atmosphere of warmth and inclusivity, where every individual feels valued and cherished. Let's embrace the beauty of kindness, fostering a culture of compassion and empathy within our communities. Let's aspire to be the kind of neighbours we would want to have – always ready to lend a helping hand, share a kind word, and spread warmth and goodwill wherever we go. Some acts of kindness you may like to try –

- Buy a pay it forward coffee
- Bake some cookies for a neighbour
- Mow a neighbour's lawn
- Cook a meal for a mum in need of a break
- Donate blood
- Give a compliment
- Leave a positive note in a library book

- Take 15 minutes to really listen to someone
- Text someone good morning and gratitude
- Share a friend's business
- Buy local
- Babysit
- Wash a friend's dishes
- Leave a note and block of chocolate in a mail box

HIKE

What a better way to celebrate nature and her cycles of life other than to be immersed in nature . Go for a hike or plan a picnic, take a flask of hot chocolate or tea. Some hikes have campgrounds close by where you can have a fire. We love to go visit our local one, go on a hike and come back for a fire to cook sausages, make some hot chocolate and roast a few marshmallows. There is always so much magic to be found in nature, you just have to look! You may even find some mossy trolls, or a fairy house in an old tree.

WINTER GATHERING

Why not gather your friends, family and community together to celebrate the days getting shorter, the nights growing longer, and the return of the sun in the days leading up to the Winter Solstice. It is a celebration that inspires a connection to community, the rhythms of nature, and the light within. A lantern walk could become part of your yearly rhythm; a ritual to bring reverence for the season to children and adults alike. You and your loved ones would gather around together to share in a feast! Afterwards, you would walk out into the night on a lantern walk, singing songs. On these walks, feelings of nurture and warmth fills us, and a comforting memory of what once was brings light deep into our hearts. Set a date, and find a place that will allow a fire and has a bit of space for a spiral. If you don't have the space at home, is there a nearby park or campground you could use? Organise with others to bring a seasonal pot luck dinner to share. Gather some foliage to create a spiral on the ground big enough to walk in and out of. Once darkness has fallen, light your lanterns and begin your walk. You may like to walk around the block or local park, or just down the driveway. Wherever you start, be sure to end at the spiral. It is lovely for everyone to stand around the spiral and sing as each child and their family enters the spiral, and leaves their lantern behind. This symbolises our journey of going inwards through the cold of winter, and the returning back out for summer. Remember this is about bringing community together: work together to make it happen, and keep it simple.

CHARADES

Charades is all about laughter and silliness. Embrace the challenge, unleash your creativity, and enjoy the hilarious moments that come from playing charades with children, friends and loved ones. Let your imagination run wild, and get ready for a memorable game of charades. Most importantly, have fun! Each Player picks a card and keeps it to themselves. When it is their turn, they act out as best they can with no words. Sounds are ok when you are playing with little kids, as let's face it when you're playing with kids, rules sometimes fly out the window; they are mostly guidelines. While one person is acting out their card, all other players try to guess what is on their card. Once guessed, play moves on to the next player.

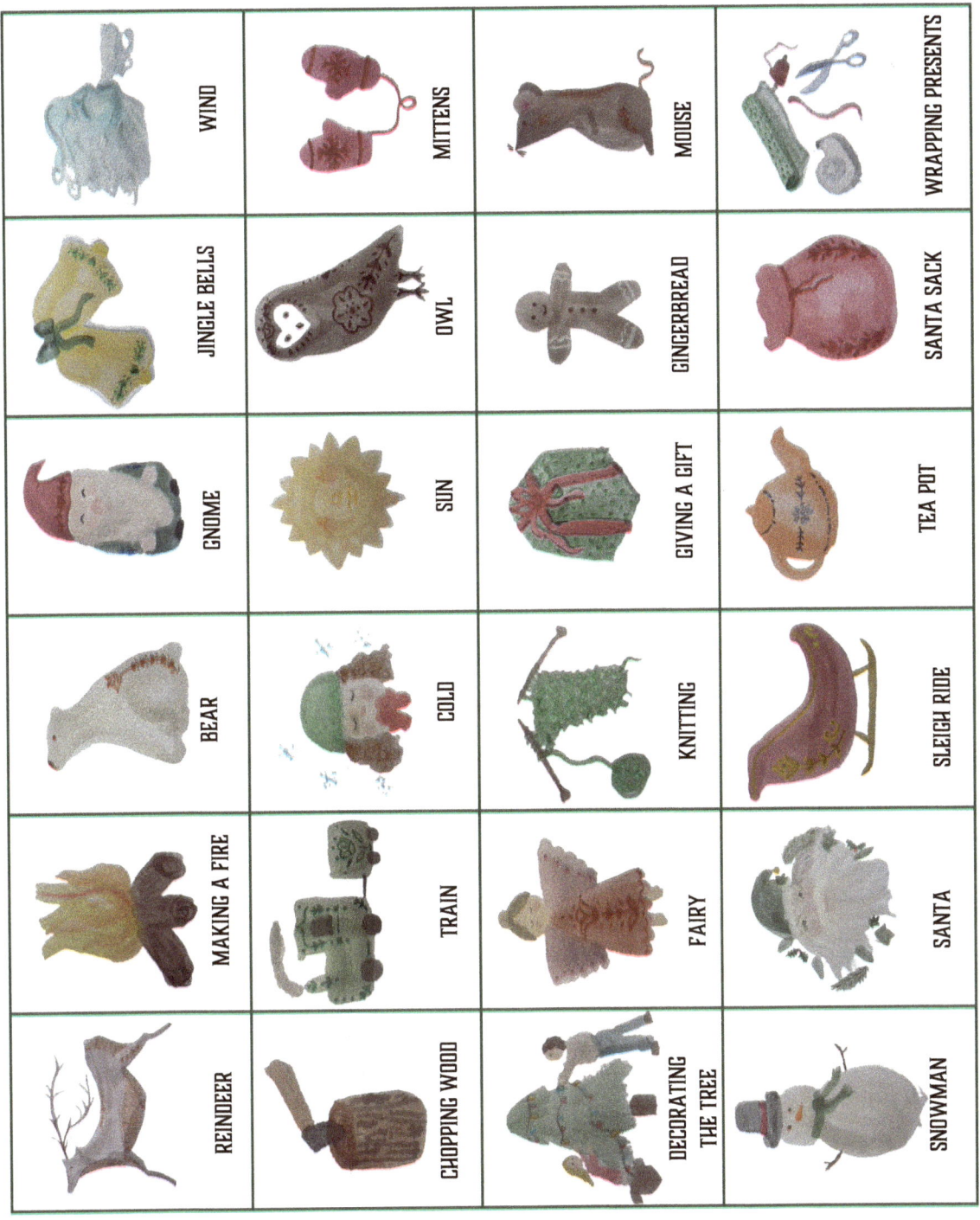

CRAFTS

PAPER CHAINS

- Stapler or glue
- Scissors
- Coloured paper: small origami squares cut in half are a good size. A similar square of an old book, magazines, or newspaper would also do the trick.

One of my only memories of my Nana is making paper chains with her. I remember the smell of the coloured paper she bought out, and how we sat on the end of the bed stapling the chains together. It's moments like these that we bring magic into our children's lives, and make the holidays memorable. Paper chains are perfect for the Yule Tree, or you can hang it along walls, across doorways, or around windows for a festive touch. Start by selecting your coloured paper. You can use one colour for a uniform look or mix and match different colours for a vibrant and festive chain. Measure and cut your paper into strips. The width of the strips will determine the thickness of your paper chain. A width of around 2.5 to 5 cm (1 to 2 inches) works well, but you can adjust the size to your preference. Use a ruler and pencil to mark the strips before cutting, or simply cut by eye if you prefer. Once you have your strips of paper, take one strip and form it into a loop, overlapping the ends slightly. Secure the ends together with glue, tape or staples to create your first chain link. Take another strip of paper and thread it through the first loop before forming it into a loop of its own. Secure the ends to create the second link in your chain. Repeat this process, alternating colours if desired, until you have a chain of the desired length.

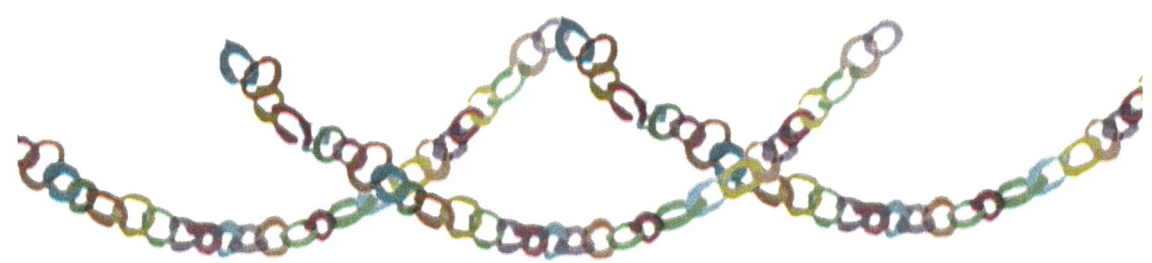

- Paper
- Scissors

SNOW FLAKES

You can go crazy with snow flakes there is no end to the patterns you can create! I love sticking these on our window and seeing the early winter light filter through. Or make little ones to stick on cards or wrapping paper. Start with a square sheet of paper. If your paper is not already square, you can easily make it square by folding one corner diagonally across to the opposite edge to form a triangle. Trim off the excess paper along the straight edge to create a square. Fold the square diagonally in half to form a triangle, then fold it in half again to form a smaller triangle. You should now have a smaller triangle with three layers of paper. With the longest side of the triangle facing you, use your scissors to cut small shapes along the folded edges of the triangle. These can be simple shapes like triangles, circles, or squares, or more intricate designs like curves and swirls. Be creative! Just be careful not to cut all the way to the opposite edge, as you want the layers to remain connected. You can mark out your pattern on your folded paper before cutting or you can live life dangerously like me and cut randomly. Unfold the paper carefully to reveal your snowflake. You may need to gently separate the layers and adjust any areas that are stuck together.

ORANGE POMANDER

- Oranges (you can also use other citrus fruits like lemons or limes)
- Cloves
- Ribbon or decorative string
- Toothpick or skewer (optional)

You can go crazy with snowflakes; there is no end to the patterns you can create! I love sticking these on our window and seeing the early winter light filter through. Or make little ones to stick on cards or wrapping paper. Start with a square sheet of paper. If your paper is not already square, you can easily make it square by folding one corner diagonally across to the opposite edge to form a triangle. Trim off the excess paper along the straight edge to create a square. Fold the square diagonally in half to form a triangle, then fold it in half again to form a smaller triangle. You should now have a smaller triangle with four layers of paper. With the longest side of the triangle facing you, use your scissors to cut small shapes along the folded edges of the triangle. These can be simple shapes like triangles, circles, or squares, or more intricate designs like curves and swirls. Be creative! Just be careful not to cut all the way to the opposite edge, as you want the layers to remain connected. You can mark out your pattern on your folded paper before cutting, or you can live life dangerously like me and cut randomly. Unfold the paper carefully to reveal your snowflake. You may need to gently separate the layers and adjust any areas that are stuck together.

WRAPPING PAPER

- Potatoes or cookie cutters
- Knife
- Acrylic paints
- Plain wrapping paper or kraft paper

Cut the potatoes in half width wise to create flat surfaces for stamping. You can also cut a little handle on the back by cutting a right angle on each side of the potato leaving enough for little hands to grab. Use a knife to carve your desired design or pattern into the flat surface of the potato. You can create simple shapes like the sun, stars, hearts, or trees. Try geometric patterns, or alternatively get more intricate with your designs. If you're not confident in your carving skills, you can use cookie cutters to help shape the potato stamps. Dip your potato stamps into acrylic paint, making sure to coat the carved surface evenly with paint. Be creative, use multiple colours of paint or stick to traditional colours such as red, green, gold and white. Carefully press the potato stamps onto the plain wrapping paper, newspaper or kraft paper. You can stamp randomly across the paper to create a scattered pattern (if you are doing this activity with kids, it will definitely be random!), or arrange the stamps in a specific pattern. Continue stamping until you've covered the entire surface of the paper with your design. Once you've finished stamping, allow the paint to dry and then get wrapping!

YULE CARDS

- Cardstock or heavy paper in various colours
- Scissors
- Glue stick
- Felt tip pens, coloured pencils, or pens for decorating
- Stamps, ink pads, stickers, glitter, or other embellishments. Go wild !
- Envelopes (if mailing the cards)
- Old Yule cards or wrapping paper
- Cheesy or non-cheesy family photo (optional)

I have always dreamt of doing some fun, tacky family Yule photo that is wonderfully staged with themed jumpers for us and the dogs. It hasn't happened yet, but maybe when the kids are older and can all sit still for a photo it will happen. If you do it, please send me one! The possibilities are endless of what you can do with some paper, glue and pencils. Creating Yule cards is a meaningful way to celebrate the magic of winter solstice by connecting with loved ones that may live far away. Fold your cardstock or heavy paper in half to create the base of your card. You can use pre-made blank cards, or cut your own from larger sheets of paper using scissors or a paper trimmer. Once you have your card base, it's time to decorate! Get creative with your designs, incorporating symbols and imagery associated with Yule and the winter solstice. Ideas include evergreen trees, holly, ivy, snowflakes, suns, moons, stars, candles, and seasonal animals like reindeer or birds. Use felt tip pens, pencils, or pens to draw and colour your designs directly onto the front of the card. You can also cut out shapes and images from coloured paper or old yule cards and glue them onto the card. Add additional embellishments to your cards to enhance their beauty and festive appeal. Consider using stamps and ink pads to add texture and patterns, or add stickers, glitter, or sequins for extra sparkle. Don't forget to add some blessings and season's greetings in the inside of your card. Share the joy of winter solstice with your thoughtful and personalized cards. They will spread warmth and cheer during the holiday season!

CRACKERS

These are one of my favourite way to either wrap a tiny gift or just add something special to the table. I love to put in some questions, charades or silly activities in to invite play and connection.

What is your favourite Yule song?

What is your favourite Yule smell?

What is your favourite memory from past Yule celebrations?

If you could have one Yule wish what would it be?

Rap jingle bells

- Toilet paper tubes (one tube per cracker)
- Coloured or patterned wrapping paper
- Cracker snaps (available at craft stores or online)
- Small trinkets or gifts (such as lollies, toys, or miniature ornaments, crystals, lip gloss)
- Ribbon or string
- Scissors
- Tape or glue
- Optional: hats and jokes or questions

 Start by gathering your materials, and deciding what small gifts or treats you'd like to include inside your crackers. Cut a piece of wrapping paper large enough to wrap around the tube completely, with a little extra length on each end to twist and tie the ends closed. Roll each tube in the wrapping paper, making sure the snap is positioned along the length of the cracker inside the toilet paper tube. Secure the wrapping paper with tape or glue, ensuring that it is tightly wrapped around the tube. Place a cracker snap inside each tube. Twist one end of the wrapping paper and tie it closed with a piece of ribbon or string. This will create one end of the cracker. Fill your cracker with your chosen gifts and treats. Close the open end of the cracker by twisting the wrapping paper and tying it closed with ribbon or string. Make sure both ends are securely sealed so that the gifts and treats remain hidden inside until the cracker is pulled open.

WREATH

- Floral wire
- Greenery
- Decorative elements such as ribbons, flowers or ornaments
- Secateurs or scissors

Making a wreath is a creative process, so don't be afraid to experiment with different materials and designs to make it uniquely yours! Start by collecting your greenery. I find smaller new growth branches work best. Once you have finished collecting, give them all a good soak for at least a few hours to help keep them hydrated and so they last longer. Trim branches to smaller lengths. Place two pieces overlapping each other and start to wrap your wire around, fastening the wire at the start with a little twist. Continue adding more branches, overlapping and wrapping with wire until you get your desired length. Bring the ends together, overlapping and wrapping the wire, and secure with another twist. Now you can start threading in and filling out your wreath. Use more wire to secure any other decorations like pine cones, dried orange, ribbon etc. Find your creativity and experiment with different arrangements until you achieve the desired look. Once you're satisfied with your wreath, take a step back and inspect it for any loose pieces or gaps. Make any necessary adjustments, and then work out the best place for a ribbon for hanging. Hang your wreath on a door, wall, gate or wherever you'd like to display it. You can use a wreath hanger or a piece of ribbon to hang it securely. You can extend the life of your wreath by spraying it with a clear sealant designed for preserving foliage. This will help keep the greenery looking fresh for longer. Sit back and admire your creation! Your handmade wreath is now ready to bring a touch of seasonal cheer to your home. You can use this same process to make a garland: just keep going to the desired length, and don't join the ends. These can be hung over doorways or placed along tables.

TIN CAN LANTERN

- Clean, empty tin can
- Hammer
- Nail
- Marker or pencil
- Tea light candle or LED candle
- Wire for the handle

Prepare your tin can, making sure that the can is clean and dry. Remove any labels or adhesive residue from the can. Use a marker or pencil to sketch out the design or pattern you want to create on the tin can. Traditional designs like stars, hearts, or simple geometric shapes work well. With the tin can placed on a sturdy surface, use the hammer and nail to carefully punch holes along the lines of your design. Space the holes evenly and keep them small to create a twinkling effect when the lantern is lit. Just make sure to leave space in between your holes so as not to "cut" out your design. Create a handle by punching two small holes opposite each other near the top edge of the tin can. Cut a piece of wire to your desired length, then thread each end through the holes and twist to secure. Ensure the handle is sturdy enough to support the weight of the lantern. Once your design is complete, place a tea light candle or LED candle inside the tin can. Light the candle and enjoy the warm, flickering glow of your home-made lantern! Place it indoors or outdoors (away from flammable materials) to create a cozy atmosphere. You may like to gather friends and family and go for a lantern walk in the dark to celebrate the return of the sun. To do this, create a spiral on the ground out of greenery – it needs to be big enough to walk in and out of. Everyone walks in procession towards the centre, leaving their lanterns somewhere along their journey in the spiral. This symbolises the journey we all go, as we turn inwards through the cold of winter and the returning back out for summer. See more on about lantern walks on page 22.

GLASS JAR LANTERN

- Glass jar
- Paste glue
- Glue brush
- Pressed flowers
- Tissue paper
- Eco glitter
- Wire or twine for handle

Prepare your jar by removing any labels or adhesive residue, and making sure that it is clean and dry. Paint a layer of glue on the jar, and while the paint is still wet, attach your decorations. Depending on the size of your jar, you may want to work in sections, so your glue does not dry before you place your decorations. You can create a scene with tissue paper, such as a winter woodland or night sky, or alternatively you can do a placement of flowers. Once you have completed your decorations, you will want to seal them with another layer of glue. Once the glue is completely dried, it is time to attach your handle. Securely attach some twine or wire around the mouth of the jar, to create a loop for the handle. Now all is left is to place a candle inside and head out for a lantern walk. See more about lantern walks on page 22.

MAKE YULE FAIRY OR ELF

- Egg carton
- Twine or yarn
- Wooden beads
- Hot glue gun
- Light cardboard
- Dried flowers
- Eco glitter
- Paint
- Felt tip pen
- Craft glue

Add a little bit more magic to the Yule Tree or around the house with these special little fairies and elves. To make these we are going to use the pyramid part in the middle of your egg carton. Cut it as long as you can, as this will be the body of your little creature. If your cardboard pyramid doesn't already have a hole in the top, carefully create a hole using your scissors. Measure a piece of twine or yarn four times the length of your body, then double it over and cut. Thread the folded end up through the wide end of the body, and poke it through the hole at the top. Thread the string through a bead to create the head. Continue to pull your twine or yarn through the head until it is long enough for hanging: about a body length above the head is perfect. Then secure it in place with some hot glue. The dangly pieces of yarn or twine will become the creature's legs. Decide how long you want its legs to be and trim them to size. Use smaller beads for the feet, securing them to the bottom of the twine or yarn with some more hot glue. Now it is time to decorate and add character to your little creature. If you would like to add wings, cut a 3cm by 8cm piece of card, and fold it back and forth like a fan. Glue one side down by placing a drop of glue at the top of the wing, then open out the far bottom corner by pinching the top edge into the body at the top of the wing placement. Decorate with dried flowers, eco glitter or paint. Use a fine felt tip pen to create the face. There you have it! You have created a little creature to add a little more fun to your festive season.

CITRUS PEEL GARLANDS

- Small cookie cutters
- Citrus peels
- Needle and thread

These look really cute hanging on the tree, or alternatively they can be used for decorating a wreath. As a bonus, it is also a great way to use up your citrus peels. When you are gathering your peels, try to keep them in larger sizes. Use your cookie cutters to cut shapes out of your peels. Once you have collected a good amount, you can start threading. With your needle and thread, go up through the back of your peel and then back down again. Repeat these steps for each piece of peel, leaving your desired space in between (roughly around 5cm—10cm). Be sure to leave a tail of thread at each end to tie a loop if you desire to hang it. Hang it somewhere dry and warm, for example, near the fire place. This makes sure that the peels dry, so as not to go mouldy. Another option to do is to thread popcorn. Good luck doing it before all the popcorn is all eaten!

PAPER BAG STARS

- Paper bags
- Glue stick
- Scissors
- Hole punch
- Twine

You may be able to find a few different sized bags at your local packaging place – they usually come in either brown or white. Otherwise, your good old lunch bag from the super market works fine. As long as the bag has a base, it will work fine. You will need 9 paper bags per star. Lay the closed paper bag with its folded bottom pointing up. Then add glue in a T shape, the top of the T goes across the bottom (closed end) of the bag. Place another paper bag directly on top of the original one, again bottom-side up. Next, repeat the process until you have used 9 bags. To create your design, you can either sketch it out first with a pencil, or alternatively you can free hand it. Avoid cutting at the bottom of the bag and too far into the middle where everything will be attached at your glue lines. If you have a good pair of scissors, you can cut two to three bags at one time, or potentially all nine. Children may prefer to cut them individually. Once you've glued and cut the nine bags together, repeat the T shaped glue on the last bag. Pull that bag and the bag on the other end towards one another, and secure by holding them together. The easiest way to do this is to place your hands inside the two bags, pressing them together until the glue dries. In the seam where they come together, use a hole punch to add a holes at the top. This will be used for hanging. Thread your twine through and secure with a knot. Your paper star is ready for hanging!

RECIPES

ELDERBERRY SYRUP

Ingredients

- 1 1/2 cup fresh Elderberries
- 3 cups Water
- 1 teaspoon ground Cinnamon
- 1 teaspoon ground Clove
- 1 tablespoon Fresh Ginger
- 1 cup Raw Honey

Elderberry syrup is said to have a long list of benefits . These include helping to boost the immune system, anti-inflammatory effects, supporting healthy skin and many more. It's easy to find by foraging; if you don't own a tree, there is bound to be someone you know with a tree in their backyard. Once you have finished harvesting, rinse the elderberry clusters under cold water to remove any dirt or debris. You can then use them immediately, or store them in the refrigerator for a few days. Alternatively, you can freeze the berries for longer-term storage. Add to a sauce pan with the water and simmer on a low heat until the liquid has reduced by about a third. Strain through a fine strainer, squishing the berries as you go. Let the liquid cool a little, and then add your spices and enjoy the aroma. Once cooled completely, add the honey and stir until it has combined together. I pour both into a jar with a tightly fitting lid, and get the kids to give it a good shake . As we all know, kids like to taste test things. The syrup will last up to 2 – 3 months refrigerated or place in the freezer. Elderberries should be cooked before consuming, as raw elderberries can cause stomach upset.

GINGER BREAD PANCAKES

- 1 1/4 cups Milk
- 6 Dates
- 1 1/2 cups Oat flour
- 3 teaspoons ground Ginger
- 1 teaspoon ground Cinnamon
- Pinch of ground Cloves
- teaspoon Baking Powder
- 2 Eggs
- Butter for frying

My kids love ginger bread pancakes. Get fancy, and add some toppings if you like. The options are endless, but some suggestions are stewed apples with pecans, bacon or berries.. Heat the milk and dates in a sauce pan over a low heat, and gently simmer until the dates are softened. Using a blender or hand-held blender, blend the milk and dates until smooth, then set aside to cool. Add all the dry ingredients to a bowl, and mix together. Whisk in the egg, followed by the milk and date mixture. Whisk well until fully combined. Place a pan on a medium to high heat. Melt your butter in the pan, and add your mix. They will cook in around 3 minutes each side. We sometimes like to make ours in a waffle pan and either way works great. Of course, don't forget the maple syrup!

GINGER BREAD PEOPLE

- 200g Oat flour
- 35g Cornflour
- 40g Butter
- 1 Egg
- 40g Brown sugar
- 40g Honey
- 1/4 teaspoon of Salt
- 6 teaspoons Ground ginger
- 2 teaspoons Nutmeg
- 2 teaspoons Cinnamon
- 1/4 teaspoon White pepper

ICING

- 150g Icing sugar
- 1 Egg white
- Squeeze of Lemon juice
- Food colouring

Melt your butter and brown sugar together. Mix all dry ingredients together, then add the cooled butter, egg and sugar, and combine. Wrap the dough in baking paper and refrigerate until it hardens. You want it to be easily pliable, but not so hard that it's like a rock. Roll out the dough, and cut out your shapes. Then continue to roll the scraps of dough together until you have cut all your cookies. Bake in the oven for 20 minutes at 175 degrees Celsius, or gas mark 4. For the icing, mix all ingredients together and either pop into a piping bag or use spoons to decorate your cookies.

As a little girl, a family friend would make the most magical ginger bread house. I remember the feeling of excitement when the house would be delivered wrapped in cellophane, tied with a bow and filled with lollies. If you are up for a challenge and want to bring some extra magic into your children's lives, I multiply this recipe by three to make enough for a gingerbread house. You can pick up gingerbread house cookie cutter sets online or at your local kitchen shop. As an alternative to a house, train cookie cutters are also available. I know that as a mum, giving that many lollies to my children makes me cringe, so I fill it with popcorn instead.

WINNIE'S APPLE CRUMBLE

- 1 kg Apples —see what's in season - you can also add, rhubarb, blackberries, or pears.
- 100g Oats
- 100g Pecans, crumbled
- 100g Oat flour - I whiz up oats in the food processor to make oat flour
- 100 g cold Butter
- Thumb size piece of Ginger, grated
- 2 Teaspoons Cinnamon
- Pinch of salt

This is a family favourite at our house and my daughter Winnie loves to make it so often that it is now fondly called Winnie's apple crumble. She's not keen to stray from plain apple crumble, but she will entertain me occasionally and add some blackberries (my favourite), rhubarb, pears, or whatever is in season and in abundance! This is also a great way to use up those apples that someone has taken one bite out of and moved on - we all know that little person! Heat the oven to 190C/170 fan/gas 5. Pop your apples in your baking dish, and sprinkle over 1 teaspoon of cinnamon Then drizzle the honey over the top, and flatten the apples down with your hand to prevent too much crumble falling through. In a separate bowl, mix your oats, flour, butter, sugar, grated ginger and pinch of salt with your fingertips until it comes together as crumble. Pour the crumb mix over the apples to form a pile in the centre, then even out. Gently press the surface so the crumble holds together and goes crisp. By leaving a few rough spots, the top will go nice and crispy. You can also achieve the same result by using a fork to rough it up a little. Pop the dish into a preheated oven for 35-40 minutes, or until the top is golden and the apples feel very soft. Leave to cool for 10 minutes before serving. Don't forget to add some double cream or ice cream!

STAINED GLASS COOKIES

- 200g Oat flour
- 35g Cornflour
- 40g Butter
- 1 Egg
- 40g Brown sugar
- 40g Honey
- 1/4 teaspoon Salt
- 1 teaspoon Vanilla essence
- Coloured boiled sweets, crushed. Use a mortar and pestle or place the sweets in a bag or tea towel, and hit them with a rolling pin.
- Cookie cutters: both big and small
- String

Melt your butter and brown sugar together over low heat. In a bowl, mix all dry ingredients together, then add the egg and cooled butter /sugar mixture, and combine. Wrap in baking paper, and refrigerate until it hardens. You want it still to be pliable but not as hard as a rock. Roll out your dough until it is about 5mm thick, and then cut out your shapes. Keep rolling your dough together, cutting out cookies, until there is none left. Use a smaller cutter to cut out shapes in your cookies. Pop them onto a tray lined with baking paper, and fill the cut outs with the crushed sweets. You can also pop a hole at the top of your cookies to hang them on your own Yule Tree, or someone else's if they are to be a gift. Bake in the oven for 15minutes at 175C / gas mark 4. Once cooked, let them cool completely on the tray. If you added a hole for hanging, thread some string through and hang them on the tree - but not for long, as they are best eaten the same day. If they are stored in a container, they will keep fresh for up to a week. But who are we kidding! They won't last that long!

HOT CHOC

Nothing better than sipping a hot chocolate on a cold day. This recipe makes enough for four. Pop all ingredients (cold) into your saucepan, and give the mixture a good whisk. Then heat it on a low heat, whisking every so often to make sure your chocolate gets mixed in, and not stuck to the bottom. Heat to your desired temperature. I like mine piping hot to melt my marshmallows!

- 1 Litre of Milk
- 3 Egg yolks
- 3 tablespoons Gelatine
- 1/4 teaspoon Salt
- 1 teaspoon Cinnamon
- 100g Chocolate - I find choc chips work well
- Optional if you are feeling fancy - marshmallows, mini candy canes, sprinkles, double cream (You can freeze a 2cm layer of double cream in a tray, then cut out with a cookie cutter)

SPICED MEAD

- 1 part Honey
- 4 parts Water
- Spices such as cinnamon sticks, gloves, ginger
- Orange peel

Mix the honey and water in a wide mouth jar or ferment pot, then cover with a cloth or tea towel. Give it a good stir with a wooden spoon about five times a day or every time you walk past it. Repeat this every day for about 5 days; it should get frothy on top, and you may see bubbles. Keep stirring about 3 times a day for another 5 days. Pour into bottles with a good sealing lid, then add your spices and leave to sit . The bubbles will develop in about a week or two. Strain it, re-bottle and then refrigerate it. If you are patient, let it age for another week or two, or if you can't wait, drink it straight away! The drink will contain a little alcohol. How much will depend on your fermenting process; the longer it is fermented, or the warmer the temperature, the higher the alcohol level. So, use your discretion around serving it to children.

GIFTS

GIFTS

Handmade gifts are such a wonderful thing. In a world filled with mass-produced items, there's an undeniable magic in the uniqueness of handmade gifts. They are not just objects; they are manifestations of love and care, creativity, and human connection. Each stitch, thought, or production carries the imprint of its creator's hands and heart, making it truly special.

Handmade gifts transcend mere material value. They embody the giver's thoughtfulness, as they invest time, skill, and passion into crafting something meaningful. Whether it's a knitted scarf, a hand drawn card, or a piece of pottery, each creation tells a story – a narrative woven with intention and love.

Receiving a handmade gift is like receiving a piece of someone's soul. They offer deeper connections between people. They bridge the gap between giver and receiver, forging bonds of appreciation and gratitude. When someone receives a handmade gift, they are not just receiving an object; they are receiving a piece of someone's heart – a token of friendship, love, and admiration. It's a tangible expression of affection, thoughtfulness. Knowing that someone dedicated their time to create something specifically for you imbues the gift with a sense of warmth and significance that cannot be replicated by anything store-bought. It reminds us to slow down, to savour the process, and to cherish the moments spent in thoughtful creation.

That I think is the point of this celebration. What a beautiful tradition to hand down to our children

Gifts don't need to be big or extreme. Lets start to normalise beautiful gifts such as delicious jams, hand made ornaments or cookies.

ROCKY ROAD

- 50g Nuts, Pistachios, pecans
- 25g Desiccated coconut flakes
- 25g Dried Ginger
- 50g Dried fruit, such as cranberries, citrus,
- 75g Treats, such as Turkish Delight, Marshmallows, Ginger Bread Cookies, Popcorn
- 400g Dark chocolate
- 50g Milk chocolate
- 50g White chocolate

Break up the dark chocolate into a large heatproof bowl. Place over a pan of boiling water and leave to melt. Prepare a baking tray (25cm x 30cm) with greaseproof paper. In another bowl add the popcorn, nuts, coconut, ginger, dried fruit and treats. Depending on how you like your rocky road you may want to roughly chop some of you ingredients. Combine your melted chocolate to your mixture and stir well. Pour out your mixture into the baking tray, spreading it out fairly evenly. Melt the milk and white chocolate in separate bowls or one after the other and drizzle over the rocky road. Leave in the fridge to cool for a few hours so it hardens and sets. Break or cut into random chunks. Perfect bagged up or head to the opshop and find a tin making an extra special gift.

TALLOW MOISTURISER

- Electric whisk or beater
- Small glass jars
- Minced Beef fat
- Slotted spoon
- Bees wax
- Raw local honey
- Jojoba, rosehip seed oil
- Optional - Colloidal silver
- Optional- Essential oils, geranium, lavender, frankincense

I find the best way to render your tallow is to ask your butcher to mince it. Pop your minced beef fat in a big sauce pan, cover with water, cook down until all the fat is liquified. Scoop out any meat bits left, this is great for the dogs if you have a furry friend. Let cool and the fat will set hard on top of the water. Drain the water off and add fresh water and heat again until liquefied. Repeat the heating and cooling process till your fat looks clean and doesn't smell like meat. I usually do this two to three times. Once it is clean drain the water and scrape any grimy bits left on the bottom of your tallow cake. Reheat the tallow to evaporate any left over water. Let cool in the fridge until it is getting hard but not solid. There is a sweet spot of not too soft and not too hard. You want it hard enough to hold its shape but soft enough to whip. When you are ready to whip have your bees wax melted and on hand ready to add. Add your colloidal silver (for a preservative but optional) honey, essential oils, jojoba and rose hip oil. Start to whip together and you will see it forming together like whipped cream slowly add your bees wax until all combined. Then there you have it, tallow moisturiser ready to pop in to jars for gifting.

SALVE

- 1 cup Olive oil (I use BP olive oil from the chemist less olive oil smell) or Jojoba
- 2-5 drops of Essential oil
- 3—4 tablespoons Beeswax, the more wax you add the hard salve will be
- Class jars

Salve is so easy to make and my kids love to do this, I think they feel like a witch making up potions. Salve is good for anything, baby's bums, chapped lips, mozzie bites (add some tea tree for that) dry skin you name it put salve on it! There are plenty of herbs that will help with different aliments, find what is right for you. If you have the luxury of time you can infuse your olive oil with calendula, plantain, lavender or other herbals, just strain before heating.

 Over a double boiler heat your oil and beeswax together on a low heat just enough to melt your wax. You don't want to over heat as it will reduce the quality of your oil. Let it get as cool as possible without setting as your essential oils will degrade with heat,. Mix together and pour into your jars and leave to set. Get fancy and make a little label ready to gift to a loved one.

HANGING ORNAMENTS

- Air dry clay
- Rolling pin
- Cookie cutters
- Straw
- Doily, leaves, flowers
- Stamps
- Thread
- Optional—paint

Roll out your clay around 5mm thick . If you are wanting to imprint a pattern on the surface start with your clay a little thicker. Pop your doily, leaf or flower on top and roll into you clay. Remove your doily, leaf or flower to reveal the pattern.

Once rolled out use your cookie cutters to cut your shapes . Use your straw to make a hole at the top for your hanging string. Optional, use some stamps to add a special message on the surface.

Pop on some carboard on a flat surface to dry out of the sun. If it dries to fast in the sun it will crack. Once dry you can paint or leave as is and thread a string through your ornament to hang. Once dry your vase frog will sit on top of your vase or a jar then place your flower through the holes to help them stay in place.

FIRE LIGHTERS

- Pine cones
- Dried flowers, herbs, citrus peels, pine needles, lint from your dryer
- Bees wax
- Old pot
- Old spoon
- Cardboard or newspaper

This is such a fun activity with the kids, as the messier the fire lighter, the better! This is a great project to do outside by a fire, as it could get messy. I use an old pot and spoon gathered from the op shop, as then I don't have to worry about removing the wax afterwards. Start with gathering your items - the wax sets quickly, so it is helpful to have everything within reach . If you have citrus peels (mandarins work great), you can cut them into shapes like little stars to add something a bit extra, but ripped up peels work just as well. Melt your bees wax, then dip your pine cones into the melted wax. Once dipped, take them out of the wax, and place onto your cardboard or newspaper. Sprinkle your citrus peels, herbs, pine needles, lint and flowers over the top of the dipped pine cones. Use your old spoon to drizzle some more wax over the top. Let them sit until the wax has hardened completely and then they are ready to be used to start your next fire.

ROLLED CANDLES

- Sheets of beeswax or candle rolling wax
- Wick
- Scissors
- Optional: Decorative coloured bees wax

You can use either beeswax sheets for bee hives or candle rolling wax. The candle rolling wax is a little softer and easier to work with, as the beeswax sheets need to be warm or they will break. Don't worry if they do break, just keep rolling and use the warmth of your fingers to mould the crack back together. Measure and cut your wax sheets into the desired size for your candle. Cut a piece of wick slightly longer than the width of your wax sheet. Place the wick on top of the sheet, and starting from that edge, carefully roll the wax sheet tightly around the wick. Apply gentle pressure as you roll to ensure it sticks together. Once you've rolled the entire sheet, press the end of the wax sheet onto the candle to secure it in place. Trim the excess wick, leaving about 1cm above the candle. You can get creative and decorate your rolled candle with coloured beeswax. To do this, first make shapes with your coloured wax, then press them onto the surface of the candle while the wax is still warm and pliable. That's it! Follow these steps, and you'll have beautiful homemade rolled candles to enjoy or give away as gifts.

POURED CANDLES

- Beeswax
- Wick
- Double boiler or a heatproof container and a saucepan
- Candle moulds or heatproof containers such as glass jars and tea cups, or try an orange with the flesh scooped out.
- Wick holder - skewer or icy pole stick

Cover your work surface with newspaper or a cloth to protect it from wax spills. If you're using candle moulds, make sure they are clean and dry. If you're using glass jars or other heatproof containers, ensure they are clean and have been prepped with a wick secured in the centre. To prepare your wicks, cut them to the appropriate length for your container. Make sure it's a bit longer than the height of the container to allow for trimming later. You can use a wick holder or tape to keep the wick centred at the bottom. Determine how much wax you'll need based on the size of your moulds. It's usually best to melt more wax than you think you'll need to avoid running out mid-pour. Use a double boiler or create one by placing a heatproof container filled with beeswax on top of a saucepan of simmering water. If you're using a mould, place the wick in the centre and secure it in place. You can do this by using a wick holder, or by wrapping it around a skewer or icy pole stick laid across the top of the mould. If you're using a glass jar, make sure the wick is centred and secured at the bottom. Once the beeswax is completely melted, carefully pour it into your prepared moulds or containers. Pour slowly and steadily to avoid splashing or spilling. Allow the candles to cool and harden completely. This process may take a few hours, depending on the size of your candles and the ambient temperature. Once the candles have cooled, trim the wick to about 1 cm above the surface of the wax. That's it! Enjoy the smell of the bees wax and bask in the warm, natural glow.

COUNT DOWN

The ancestors would celebrate with twelve days of Yule. This was a time of joy, renewal and community bonding, as they celebrated the turning of the seasons. They looked forward to the returning of the sun, and the promise of spring. They celebrated over the 12 days with feasting, gift giving and connecting with friends, family and community. Count downs are a really nice way to incorporate the tradition of 12 days of Yule and for children to have a grounding in the season and a sense of time. It reduces the need for the constant questions of - 'Is it Yule yet? You can choose when and how long you would like to do your family count down. You could start on the first of June/December, or you could do it over 12 days with Yule either being in the middle or at the end of the count down. This can be as simple or extravagant as you like. I have included cards for you to print, cutout or photocopy, find them on pages 58-61 . As an alternative, you can simply write them out yourself. Once you have chosen your cards, and when you would like to start your countdown, here are a few ideas on how to display them.

- A simple string with small envelopes pegged for each day

- Bunting with the activity on the back

- Hang them on the Yule tree

- Sew a wall hanging with pockets to pop each card in

I have left it open for you to be able to tailor it to your family life. There are also some blank cards for you to add your own ideas and activities. Get the calendar out, and pick the simple activities on days that are already busy, such as having a hot chocolate on a day that you have lots of errands to run. Keep the bigger ones such as gift making for free days at home. Find ways to make it a simple integration into your family life. The goal here is to bring connection, not overwhelm. If you miss a day, don't stress! We often do a missed activity on a day that is less busy, and usually by the time we get to the end, we have completed most of them. If there is one we didn't get to, that is ok, because we have had many moments of connection and the activities will be there, and can be looked forward to for next year. Returning to these activities year after year is what instils tradition in our children. and it is what creates memories and feelings of connection. Have a wonderful time with your loved ones!

MAKE HOT CHOCOLATE	DECORATE THE YULE TREE	MAKE CRACKERS
MAKE LANTERN	GO ON A HIKE	MAKE A DECORATION
MAKE A YULE FAIRY OR ELF	RANDOM ACT OF KINDNESS	PLAY CHARADES
MAKE GINGER BREAD PANCAKES	MAKE A WREATH	MAKE ORANGE POMANDERS

MAKE APPLE CRUMBLE	MAKE WRAPPING PAPER	MAKE SOME GIFTS
MAKE STAINED GLASS WINDOW COOKIES	MAKE YULE CARDS	MAKE A PAPER CHAIN
MAKE GINGER BREAD COOKIES	MAKE SNOWFLAKES	WRITE A LETTER TO SANTA

SONGS

I WALK WITH MY LITTLE LANTERN

I walk with my little lantern,

My lantern is my light.

Above the stars are shining,

And both of us are bright.

My little light please stay with me,

la bimmel, la bammel, la boom.

My little light please stay with me,

la bimmel, la bammel, la boom.

There are a few versions of this old German folk song floating around that you can search on your music streaming service to listen along to.

THE NIGHT IS COLD

The night is cold the moon is new/full

Mother loves winter and I do too

And I do too

The night is cold the moon is new/full

Father loves winter and I do too

And I do too

The night is cold the moon is new/full

Sister loves winter and I do too

And I do too

This is a beautiful little song. You can keep going to include everyone in the family either by name or using terms like brother, sister, Grandma etc.

DECK THE HALLS

Deck the halls with boughs of holly
Fa-la-la-la-la, la-la-la-la
'Tis the season to be jolly
Fa-la-la-la-la, la-la-la-la
Don we now our gay apparel
Fa-la-la, la-la-la, la-la-la
Troll the ancient Yule-tide carol
Fa-la-la-la-la, la-la-la-la

See the blazing Yule before us
Fa-la-la-la-la, la-la-la-la
Strike the harp and join the chorus
Fa-la-la-la-la, la-la-la-la
Follow me in merry measure
Fa-la-la, la-la-la, la-la-la
While I tell of Yule-tide treasure
Fa-la-la-la-la, la-la-la-la

Fast away the old year passes
Fa-la-la-la-la, la-la-la-la
Hail the new year, lads and lasses
Fa-la-la-la-la, la-la-la-la
Sing we joyous, all together
Fa-la-la, la-la-la, la-la-la
Heedless of the wind and weather
Fa-la-la-la-la, la-la-la-la

JINGLE BELLS

Dashing through the snow
In a one-horse open sleigh
O'er the fields we go
Laughing all the way
Bells on bobtails ring
Making spirits bright
What fun it is to ride and sing
A sleighing song tonight

Oh! Jingle bells, jingle bells
Jingle all the way
Oh, what fun it is to ride
In a one-horse open sleigh, hey
Jingle bells, jingle bells
Jingle all the way
Oh, what fun it is to ride
In a one-horse open sleigh

Shelley is a mother of three, an artist and is passionate about ancestorial rituals. She enjoys supporting others to connect with their loved ones, and bring reverence for the seasons, into their lives. She's a beacon of creativity and resilience. Balancing the demands of parenthood with her passion for creativity, she brings a unique perspective to her work. Most days you will find her home schooling her children and fitting in as much creativity as she can. She also supports women in her community by facilitating women's circles with a focus of bringing joy back to motherhood.

www.ingramcontent.com/pod-product-compliance
Lightning Source LLC
Chambersburg PA
CBHW061122070526
44583CB00028B/3356